D1179075

KATHLEEN PARTRIDGE'S

Book of Friendship and

Flowers

To

....

From

....

Jarrold Colour Publications, Norwich.

Mingling amongst the snowdrops, the aconite
symbolises misanthropy

(Someone who has an irrational
hatred or distrust of people
- in general)

THE MESSAGE

*When petals fall the flowers speak
With every bouquet spent.
They speak of love and friendship
Through the subtlety of scent.*

*Of hope and peace and happiness
Of courage, joy or fear
Each petal sends a message
To the one who cares to hear.*

*And those who love and those who part
And those who only wait
Will find their message woven
In the tapestry of Fate.*

The dainty snowdrop signifies hope

THE COMING OF FRIENDS

We long for you and look for you
In wintry winds and rain
Waiting for your visit
To make us young again.

Forsythia, grape hyacinths
And hawthorn down the dell
All of them will blossom
In time to wish you well.

Catkins in the copses
And voilets in the hollow
Carpeting the footpaths
For friendly feet to follow.

One of the first signs of spring, the crocus denotes
youthful gladness

The grape hyacinth, otherwise known as muscari

Wild daffodils in Kilcot Wood, Newent, Gloucestershire

COME OUT TO PLAY

When the air vibrates with springtime
Budding leaves replace the old
And hearts grow light with promise
As the earth spills out her gold.

And so arrive the daffodils
In glorious array
To call us and enthrall us
And to take our breath away.

The much loved common daffodil, or trumpet narcissi

Primroses and daffodils create a harmonious blend of
spring colour

FAITHFUL TO THE SPRING

Lord who made the fields and flowers
And set the sky with stars alight
Who rinsed the earth in dew and showers
To wash the narcis extra white,

Lord who brought a world of wonder
And set the silver in the blue
Break the hardened soil asunder
To bring the speedwell shining through.

Hidden amongst primroses and daisies, speedwell
signifies fidelity

BE HAPPY FRIEND

The flowers that springtime promised
Have bloomed in winter's wake
Old troubles grow less wearisome
And hearts forget to ache.

Maybe love lies bleeding
But the flax will never fail
And orchids are a miracle
That make the sun turn pale.

The scilla bells are ringing
With the sweetest music yet
Calling all who listen
To forgive and to forget.

In between dwarf tulips, the polyanthus denotes confidence

Some superb blooms of the orchid burgundian

The primrose signifies early youth

Primroses and periwinkles
Violets and views
Palm and polyanthus
In the daily news.

Youngest of the springtime
Open faces, starry eyes
Turning to the world
A look of permanent surprise.

The young at heart will gather
And arrange them in a bowl
Because they treasure secrets
But they never tell a soul.

The violet odorata, so named because of its distinctive scent

EVERYDAY FRIENDS

Saxifrage called London pride
An easy growing one.
Contented in the shade
As it is happy in the sun.

When mixed with high or humble blooms
As neighbourly and nice
Growing in abundance
And never thinking twice.

Like kindly friends and neighbours
Always near to bear the brunt
As happy in the back row
As they would be in the front.

Irish saxifrage or saxifraga rosacea

Pasque flower or pulsatilla vulgaris

FAIRY FLOWERS

Perfect are the petals on a palette leaf of green
Poised like fairy wings embroidered for the fairy queen.
These cyclamens called 'diffident' are shy, but not forlorn,
Shiny as the sunset and as delicate as dawn.
Isn't it amazing how the petals are uncurled.
To think that we awake to find such beauty in the world!

The cyclamen symbolises diffidence

Dainty flowers of the cyclamen neapolitanum

The tulip symbolises hopeless love

STRENGTH FOR THE DAY

A gift of tulips is a loving token
A feeling of affection never spoken
So long to last, so sturdy to behold
In pink or purple, multi-toned or gold.

Though massed by millions in the tulip fields
A few set in a vase much pleasure yields
So will affection blossom in the room
With strength for the day in every upright bloom.

Tightly-packed, these tulips still stand proud

Harewood House and gardens, Yorkshire

REMEMBER ME

Gracious garden tended
By the love of many hands
Years of thought have blended
Where the weeping willow stands.

The old house gazes downwards
From her windows near the sky
And hopes the world remembers her
When time has passed her by.

There's virtue in the soil
That has been turned by countless spades
And in earth's heart a seed is dropped
By every flower that fades.

The forget-me-not stands for true love

CARPET OF BLUE

Bluer than a sailor's eyes
Bluer than the bluest skies
Spread your carpet, ring your bells
Round the trees and down the dells.

Call a meeting place for friends
In the woods where anger ends.
Tell two hearts for truelove's sake
To keep the loving vows they make.

Though trains may whistle, traffic roar
And aircraft in the heavens soar
Though houses rise and cities fall
The bluebells grow in spite of all.

These vivid bluebells denote constancy

Bluebell woods of Lower Hardres, near Canterbury, Kent

A superb array of azaleas in Leonardslee Gardens, Sussex

FLOWERS FROM THE EAST

In far off lands discoveries
Were made by pioneers
Strange plants, strange foods, strange animals
Were brought home through the years.

Azaleas were also brought
From India and Japan
And all this loveliness
Grows from the forethought of one man.

Reflections of rhododendrons in Sheffield Park, Sussex

BE HAPPY NOW

Unaware the little lily
Of our love and our affection
She snuggles in the shadow of a leaf
For her protection.

Too shy to ring her bell
And boast the beauty of her birth
Yet the perfume of her petals
Is the sweetest scent on earth.

No wonder that the hearts will bleed
That overhang her shelter
And the musk will cuddle closer
In the hope that he may melt her.

The exotic hemerocallis, or day lily

Lily of the valley denotes a return of happiness

The lupin symbolises voraciousness

LONERS

Big and bright and beautiful
The other flowers they shun
Unlike the genial lupin
Who is friends with everyone.

Like to the hardy people
Who are purposeful and proud
Who bloom in sunny solitude
Yet wither in a crowd.

The gaily coloured lupin brightens many an English garden

ROSES, ROSES EVERYWHERE

In the heart of every rose
A pearl of dew prepares to settle
Eternal summer lingers
In the texture of a petal.

A rose will grace a mansion
Her intrusion needs no pardon
She is equally at home
In any little cottage garden.

A perfect specimen of the silver jubilee rose

A charming rose-covered cottage in Adlestrop,
Gloucestershire

The magnificent velvet hour rose

FLOWERS FOR A CHILD

Daisy white you look so pert
In your spotless frilly skirt.
Innocent, and yet I wist
By the crimson roses kissed.

Daisy pied and starry eyed
Carmine lips to you are plied
All the children know your name
Yet the roses blush for shame.

Growing winsome, growing wild
Just the keepsake for a child
Whose joy and laughter you must share
To make a daisy chain to wear.

These wild daisies signify innocence

JOURNEY WITH JOY

Such a ponderous name for a beautiful flower
That shines in the dark at the midnight hour.
On African nights in the heat and the dust
When there's no one to turn to and no one to trust.

A flower of such beauty it hardly seems real
Of perfect proportion and special appeal
The star of the Veldt, making travellers aware
That God guards us all from His heaven up there.

Pyrethrums, more simple, but sturdier yet
Are a flower that we pluck and as quickly forget.
So like any daisy, a friend for the day
Sent to bless us, caress us, and lighten our way.

The dimorphotheca or star of the veldt

Standing tall is the pyrethrum roseum 'Brenda'

The ever-popular sweet pea is otherwise called
lathyrus odoratus

OLD FASHIONED FLOWERS

It's the old fashioned honeysuckle
The common hedgerow kind
That has the sweetest smell
And leaves a memory behind.

It's the old fashioned sweet peas
Like baby butterflies
That fill the room with fragrance
And entrance our waking eyes.

Honeysuckle symbolises devoted affection

SHADES OF PURPLE

Colour of an autumn sky
Where pink and purple clouds race by
Bringing happy thoughts to those
Who make the most of summer's close.

Likewise the iris, set in green
Royal purple as a queen
'Raise your head and smile and wave'
Is that the way we should behave?

A bright display of erigeron speciosus 'Felicity'

The Water Garden, Wakehurst Place, Sussex

Water—lilies denote purity

OPENING TIME

Waterlilies on a lake
What a restful sight they make!
Flat the leaves that quiver slightly
Where the wagtails tread so lightly.

Hawks and herons come and go
Where the peaceful waters flow
When foxgloves toll for time and tide
The lilies close at eventide.

An unusual close-up of water–lilies in full bloom

Thrift clings to the cliff top at Hope Cove,
Bigbury Bay, Devon

NICKNAMES

The nicknames of the flowers
Must be as old as father time.
Pert, appealing, pretty
Set to music and to rhyme.

Thrift and grannies bonnet,
Rose of Sharon, meadow rue,
Jacob's ladder, creeping Jenny,
Shepherd's needle, bird's-eye blue.

Who named the thyme and tonguebleed,
Old man's beard, and dragonwort,
And set the ragged robin
Next to break your mother's heart?

Old man's beard, also known as traveller's joy

OVER THE WALL

The clematis must climb the wall
To see the other side.
The hollyhocks are curious too
And rosebay has a lovely view
Outgazing far and wide.
Yet none of them will beg your pardon
When they peer into your garden
Always reaching for a better view.
Such saucy flowers, although not ours.
'I'd love some in my garden ... Wouldn't you?'

The clematis symbolises mental beauty

Rosebay willow herb signifies danger

An old-fashioned cottage and garden near Benover, Kent

ALL FRIENDS TOGETHER

An old fashioned garden of old fashioned flowers,
Tansy and teasle on bankside and bowers,
A friendly profusion of lily and phlox
Carnations and cornflowers, verbena and stocks.

The pathways are peaceful, the moss is caressing,
The scent of the lavender offers a blessing
And somewhere a sundial is telling the hours
In a friendly old garden of old fashioned flowers.

These cottages have withstood the test of time –
Lustleigh in Devon

REVERENCE

No colour is so right
To clothe the lily as the white
Waxen as a candle
On the altar cloth at night.

To pluck it like a primrose
Would be sacrilege as such
She is too fair to fondle
And too beautiful to touch.

Lilium auratum or golden-rayed lily

A white lily symbolises purity

Odontoglossum, one of thousands of different species
of orchid

FROM HEAVEN TO EARTH

The sunbeams dance down from a shaft out of heaven
The perfume soars up where the lark sweetly sings
And that's why these flowers wear celestial colours
The delicate texture of angels' wings.

And deep in the heart of the sweet passion flower
The stamens are formed as the calvary cross
Stained by the blood of our Lord's crown of thorns
Marked by the tears that were shed for His loss.

Passion flower or passiflora caerulea

WINTER FRIEND

Some call it 'poison ivy'
But is is a winter friend
And stays when red hot pokers fade
And tiger lilies end.

Constant and contented
On the garden wall it grows
Sheltering the birds
From every stormy wind that blows.

Snow softens many a dull winter landscape

Clinging and irrepressible, ivy denotes fidelity

Hydrangeas in a South Milton cottage garden, Devon

MELLOW MOMENTS

Ferns for fascination
When the world is green and wild
Shelter for the little creatures
Cover for a child.

And when hydrangeas lose their hue
With petals paper thin
We know that summer's going out
And winter coming in.

Dryopteris borreri or golden–scaled male fern

HEARTSEASE

Pansy, prettiest of flowers
Open faced to sun and showers
Velvet as the backs of bees
Call them 'heartsease' if you please

And the spur of the nasturtium
Takes the bees on an excursion
Deep down in the pointed tip
We can taste it if we sip.

Grown with joy in sunny places
With every colour in their faces
Gather them before they wane
And they will quickly grow again.

A close-up reveals the pretty velvet petals of the pansy

Garden pansy or viola wittrockiana

EVERGREEN

The yew is for sorrow, but green is the leaf
Keeping its foliage even in grief.
That is the reason why yews go not bare
But point to new hope in the midst of old care.

And evergreen colours are not born to die
But decorate earth when the summer goes by
They cover the landscape while earth takes a rest
Immortal, heartlifting, and by our Lord blessed.

The immaculately maintained topiary at
Levens Hall, Cumbria

Stately yew hedges complement this majestic architecture at
Manderston, Borders

The dahlia denotes instability

LAST TO REIGN

The queen of all the gardens there she stands
While Autumn tints the world with golden hands.
Reigning alone, the dahlia rules the world
With buttons, pompons or with spikes uncurled.

And there are some that rule as if in state
With blossoms like a giant golden plate.
And those with ragged curls that sweetly swing
As if to give the earth her final fling.

A fine example of a dahlia in all its glory

BROKEN HEARTED

I bid you love remember
When you are fancy free
That not so very long ago
You were attached to me.

Chrysanthemums you sent me
Gold as the sun above
Knowing that the meaning of these flowers
Was 'slighted love'.

So press this petal in a book
And on some distant day
You'll open it to take a look
And steal my heart away.

Chrysanthemum segetum

Chrysanthemums symbolise slighted love

THE FAIREST FLOWER

The leaves are green as friendship
That lasts the winter through.
The blossoms shine on darker days
As dear friends always do.

Peace to the heart that grieves you bring
And joy to the anxious mind.
O lovely Christmas rose
Just for a friend you are designed.

Christmas rose or helleborus niger

ISBN 0-7117-0349-3 © Copyright Jarrold Colour Publications 1988. Designed and produced by Parke Sutton Limited, Norwich for Jarrold Colour Publications, Norwich. Origination by Blackfriars Colour Repro, Norwich. Printed in Portugal.